Simple American Cooking

Edited by
Evelyn L. Beilenson

Designed by
Sandra Baenen and
Ellen Witteborg

PETER PAUPER PRESS, INC.
WHITE PLAINS • NEW YORK

TABLE OF CONTENTS

A New England Menu

❖ ❖ ❖ ❖ ❖ ❖ ❖ ❖

New England Clam Chowder

Standing Rib Roast

Yorkshire Pudding

Stuffed Zucchini Squash

Apple Pie or Indian Pudding

Coffee or Tea

New England Clam Chowder

¾ cup butter
6 small onions, minced
2 pints clams, chopped
4 cups boiling water
4 potatoes, diced
Salt and pepper to taste
2 quarts milk
Oysterettes

Melt butter and fry onions until golden brown. Add chopped clams and simmer 5 or 6 minutes. Add boiling water, potatoes, salt and pepper and cook for 30 minutes. Pour in milk, heat thoroughly; serve with oysterettes.

Boiled Lobsters

2 live lobsters (1 pound each)
3 quarts boiling water
3 tablespoons salt
Melted butter

Plunge lobsters headfirst into boiling salted water. Cover and return to boiling point. Simmer for 20 minutes. Drain. Place lobster on its back. With a sharp knife cut in half lengthwise. Remove stomach, which is just back of head, and intestinal vein, which runs from stomach to tip of tail. Do not discard green liver and coral roe; they are delicious. Crack claws. Serve with melted butter.

NEW ENGLAND BOILED DINNER

4 pounds corned beef, preferably brisket
8 small white onions, peeled
8 parsnips
8 carrots
8 potatoes
1 cabbage, cored and cut in eighths
  Parsley for garnish

Wash beef under running water to remove brine. Place in large kettle, cover with cold water, bring slowly to a boil and cook 5 minutes. Remove scum, cover and simmer 2½ hours.

Skim excess fat off liquid. Then bring to a rolling boil. Add whole onions, parsnips, carrots and potatoes, and cook gently, uncovered, 20 minutes. Add cabbage and cook 20 minutes longer, or until vegetables are just tender.

Place meat on large heated platter and arrange vegetables around it. Garnish with parsley. Makes 8 servings.

STUFFED ZUCCHINI SQUASH

8   medium zucchini
4   cups soft bread crumbs
1   cup grated cheese, divided
1   medium onion, minced
3   tablespoons minced parsley
1   teaspoon salt
⅛   teaspoon pepper
2   eggs, beaten
3   tablespoons butter

Trim ends of zucchini. Cut in half lengthwise. Remove pulp with spoon and combine with bread crumbs, ¾ cup cheese, onion, parsley, salt, pepper, and eggs. Fill zucchini shells with mixture. Dot with butter and sprinkle with remaining cheese. Bake in 350 degree oven ½ hour. Makes 8 servings.

STANDING RIB ROAST

Select a 2- or 3-rib standing rib roast (4 to 5 pounds). Place fat side up in roasting pan; season with salt and pepper and place in 350 degree oven. Do not cover and do not add water.

Allow 18 to 20 minutes per pound for rare roast, 22 to 25 minutes per pound for medium, and 27 to 30 minutes per pound for well-done. Serve with Yorkshire Pudding.

YORKSHIRE PUDDING

½   cup drippings from rib roast
5   eggs
2   cups milk
2   cups flour
¼   teaspoon salt

Pour drippings from rib roast into approximately 10″ x 12″ pan. Preheat pan with fat in oven. Beat remaining ingredients until evenly blended, but do not overbeat. Pour mixture into pan and bake at 450 degrees about 30 minutes.

CHESTNUT STUFFING

     1 cup butter
     1 cup minced onion
     1 teaspoon thyme
     1 teaspoon sage
  1½ teaspoons salt
   ¾ teaspoon pepper
   ⅓ cup chopped parsley
   ¾ cup chopped celery and leaves
     8 cups soft stale bread crumbs or cubes
     1 pound Italian chestnuts, cooked, shelled
        and chopped

Melt butter in skillet and add all ingredients except bread crumbs and chestnuts. Cook 5 minutes. Add crumbs and chestnuts. Makes about 10 cups of turkey stuffing.

BREAD CRUMB STUFFING

     4 cups dry bread crumbs
     1 medium onion, chopped
     1 teaspoon salt
   ¼ teaspoon pepper
        Sage to taste
        Parsley, chopped
   ¼ teaspoon poultry seasoning
   ⅓ cup melted butter
        Hot water or stock to moisten

Combine bread crumbs, onion, and seasonings; add butter and sufficient liquid to moisten. Mix gently. Allow 1 cup stuffing for each pound of poultry or game.

ROAST TURKEY

Dress and clean turkey. Rub inside with salt and pepper. Stuff neck cavity. Fasten opening with metal pins. Fill body cavity loosely with stuffing. Rub with butter or make paste of ½ cup of butter, ¾ cup flour; spread over all parts of turkey.

Place turkey breast side down in open roasting pan to allow juices to run down into breast. Drip pan from broiler may be used if large roaster is not available. Roast uncovered in 300-325 degree oven 15 to 20 minutes per pound, turning turkey over onto back when half done.

Baste at 30-minute intervals with mixture of melted butter and hot water. When breast and legs become light brown, cover with brown paper. Turkey is done when meat pulls away from leg bones.

BOSTON BAKED BEANS

1 pound pea, marrow or navy beans
1 medium onion
½ pound salt pork
4 tablespoons brown sugar
½ teaspoon salt
  Dash pepper
1 teaspoon dry mustard
½ cup molasses
  Boiling water
1 tablespoon ketchup

Wash beans, cover with cold water and let soak overnight. Drain and set beans aside. Quarter onion and place in bottom of bean crock. Cut salt pork into chunks and place 3 or 4 pieces on top of onion. Pour beans into crock, place remainder of salt pork on top, sprinkle with sugar, salt, pepper, ketchup, and mustard, and add molasses. Add enough boiling water to cover beans. Cover and bake in 325 degree oven 5 to 6 hours or until beans are tender and brown. Keep beans covered with liquid except during last hour of baking, when water is allowed to bake away. About 30 minutes before beans are done, remove cover. Serve with brown bread. Makes 6 servings.

Boston Brown Bread

1 cup flour
1 cup corn meal
1 cup coarse wheat flour
¾ tablespoon baking soda
1 teaspoon salt
¾ cup molasses
2 cups sour milk, or 1¾ cups sweet milk
1 cup seedless raisins
Butter for greasing mold

Mix and sift dry ingredients, add molasses, milk and raisins, stir until well mixed, and fill well-greased mold not more than two-thirds full. Cover mold tightly and place mold on trivet in kettle containing boiling water, allowing water to come halfway up around mold. Cover kettle and steam 3½ hours, keeping water at boiling point. Add more boiling water as needed. Note: Boston Brown Bread may be steamed in double boiler. Grease top part and half fill with batter. Set over lower part which contains enough boiling water to cover ½ inch of base of upper part. Cover closely and steam 3 hours over low heat, keeping water at boiling point.

Apple Pie

3 pounds tart green apples
1 cup sugar
2 tablespoons flour
⅛ teaspoon salt
1 teaspoon cinnamon
¼ teaspoon nutmeg
  Pastry for double-crust pie (9-inch)
4 tablespoons butter

Peel apples and slice thin; add sugar mixed with flour, salt and spices. Fill 9-inch pastry-lined pie pan. Dot with butter. Adjust top crust. Bake at 450 degrees for 10 minutes, then at 350 degrees about 40 minutes. Makes 6 servings.

Indian Pudding

2 cups scalded milk
⅓ cup corn meal
¼ cup sugar
¼ cup butter
½ cup molasses
1 teaspoon salt
1 teaspoon ginger or cinnamon
½ cup raisins (optional)
2 cups cold milk
  Sweet cream

Pour scalded milk slowly on corn meal; cook in double boiler 20 minutes. Add sugar, butter, molasses, salt, and ginger or cinnamon, and raisins if desired. Pour into buttered pudding dish, add cold milk, set in pan of hot water, and bake 3 hours in 250 degree oven. Serve with cream.

PUMPKIN PIE

1¼ cups strained, cooked pumpkin
⅔ cup sugar
½ teaspoon salt
⅔ teaspoon ginger
1 teaspoon cinnamon
¼ teaspoon nutmeg
3 eggs, separated
1¼ cups scalded milk
1 6-ounce can (¾ cup) evaporated milk
  Pastry for single-crust pie (9-inch)

Thoroughly combine pumpkin, sugar, salt and spices. Add egg yolks and milk, and blend. Fold in beaten egg whites. Pour into 9-inch pastry-lined pie pan. Bake at 450 degrees for 10 minutes, then at 325 degrees for about 45 minutes, or until mixture does not stick to knife. Top with whipped cream, if desired. Makes 6 servings.

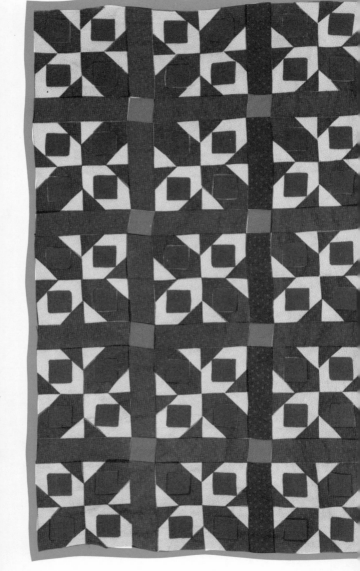

A Southern Menu

❖ ❖ ❖ ❖ ❖ ❖ ❖ ❖

Oysters Rockefeller

Celery   Olives

Corn Bread

Baked Ham

Southern Fried Chicken

Southern Black-Eyed Peas

Sweet Potato Pudding

Southern Pecan Pie

Coffee or Tea

SOUTHERN GUMBO

¼ cup chicken fat
3½ pounds chicken, cut into serving pieces
¾ pound ham, cubed
1 onion, sliced
1 cup canned sweet corn
1 cup sliced fresh okra
1 tablespoon salt
7 cups boiling water
1 pint shelled fresh oysters and liquor
1 bay leaf, crushed

Melt fat in heavy 1 gallon pot. Brown chicken and ham lightly on all sides. Add onion and cook 6 minutes. Add corn, okra, salt, and water. Cover and simmer 2 hours. Remove chicken and cut meat from bones. Return only meat to soup. Add oysters and bay leaf. Simmer 3 minutes and serve at once.

OYSTERS ROCKEFELLER

36 oysters on the half shell
Rock salt
2 cups cooked and drained spinach
¼ cup chopped scallions
2 tablespoons minced parsley
2 tablespoons finely chopped celery

½ teaspoon salt
6 drops hot pepper sauce
⅓ cup butter
2 teaspoons anisette
½ cup fine dried bread crumbs

Put oysters in their shells on a bed of rock salt so they will remain upright and not lose their juice. Combine spinach, scallions, parsley and celery. Put this mixture through a food grinder. Add salt and hot pepper sauce, mixing well. Cook mixture in butter and anisette over low heat for 4 or 5 minutes. Fold in bread crumbs and spread 1 tablespoon of mixture on each oyster. Bake in a 400 degree oven for 10 minutes or until lightly browned.

Corn Bread

1 cup corn meal
1 cup flour
3 teaspoons baking powder
½ teaspoon salt
1 egg
1 cup milk
¼ cup butter, melted
2 slices cooked bacon, crumbled

Sift together corn meal, flour, baking powder and salt. Beat egg; add milk and butter. Add egg mixture to dry ingredients, stirring just enough to moisten. Add crumbled bacon. Pour into greased 8 inch x 8 inch x 2 inch pan. Bake in 400 degree oven 30 minutes, and cut into 2½ inch squares.

SPOON BREAD

2 cups corn meal
2½ cups boiling water
1½ tablespoons butter, melted
1½ teaspoons salt
2 eggs, separated
1½ cups buttermilk
1 teaspoon baking soda

Add corn meal slowly to boiling water and let stand until cool. Add butter, salt, beaten egg yolks, buttermilk and baking soda. Beat 2 minutes and add beaten whites. Place in buttered baking dish. Bake in 400 degree oven 40 minutes. Makes 6 servings.

FRIED CHICKEN

1 fryer (2½ pounds), cut up
2 tablespoons evaporated milk
2 tablespoons water
   Seasoned flour
   Vegetable oil

Marinate chicken in water and milk
for ten minutes. Pour flour into bowl
and season with salt and pepper. Dip
chicken pieces in seasoned flour.
Shake off excess flour. Deep fry in
vegetable oil at 300 degrees or pan
fry, making sure oil is hot before put-
ting chicken in. Make sure chicken is
covered with oil at all times. Fry until
golden brown.

BAKED VIRGINIA HAM

Place ham fat side up on rack in open
roasting pan. Do not cover. Bake in
300 degree oven, without water, allowing 15 to 20 minutes per pound
for a large ham; 20 to 25 minutes per
pound for a small ham; and 25 to 30
minutes per pound for a half ham.

The shorter cooking time in each case is for tenderized hams. Meat thermometer registers 170 degrees when ham is done, 160 degrees for tenderized hams.

Ham may be basted during cooking period with honey, syrup from canned fruit, or cider. One half hour before baking is done, score fat in diamond shapes, rub surface with dry mustard and brown sugar moistened with ham drippings, and stick a whole clove in each diamond. Large ham makes 24 servings.

JAMBALAYA

3	cups rice
1	large onion, sliced
¾	cup shortening
1	slice raw ham, coarsely diced
1½	cups cooked shrimp
1½	cups canned tomatoes
1	green pepper
2	cloves garlic
	Thyme
1	bay leaf
	Salt and pepper to taste
3	cups water

Wash rice until clear. Saute onion with rice in shortening until brown. Add meat, shrimp, tomatoes and remaining ingredients except water. Stir for three minutes over low flame. Add water and cook for 30 minutes or until done. Makes 8 servings.

SWEET POTATO PUDDING

2 cups sweet potatoes, cooked
1 cup hot milk
½ teaspoon salt
2 tablespoons sugar
2 tablespoons butter
2 eggs, separated
1 tablespoon nutmeg
1 cup broken nut meats (optional)

Mash sweet potatoes thoroughly. Scald milk. Dissolve salt, sugar, and butter in milk, stirring until melted. Add this mixture to potatoes. Mix and beat until smooth. Separate eggs and beat yolks well. Add to potatoes. Add nutmeg. Beat whites of eggs until stiff. Fold whites into potatoes and pour mixture into buttered baking dish.

Place in 350 degree oven and bake until brown. Serve at once. Makes 6 servings.

Southern Black-Eyed Peas

1 medium onion
2 stalks celery
¾ pound ham hock
1½ cups water
1 pound black-eyed peas, fresh or frozen

Dice onion and celery and lightly saute until transparent. Add ham hock and lightly braise. Add water and black-eyed peas. Simmer gently for 1 to 1½ hours. Do not boil because peas are delicate and break easily. Season to taste before serving.

Wilma Jean Sloan

Candied Sweet Potatoes

6 sweet potatoes
¾ cup brown sugar
¾ cup butter
½ cup hot water

Cook sweet potatoes covered in boiling water until nearly tender. Remove potatoes from pot and peel. Slice lengthwise and place in buttered baking dish. Make syrup of brown sugar, butter, and water. Pour over potatoes and bake at 375 degrees for 25 minutes. Makes 6-8 servings.

FRIED GRITS

1   cup white or yellow grits
4   cups water
1   teaspoon salt
2   eggs
¼   cup milk
    Salt and pepper to taste
¾   cup cracker crumbs
    Vegetable oil

Boil grits in salted water for 15 minutes. Pour and spread in a buttered dish. Let stand until thoroughly cold, then cut into three-inch squares. Beat eggs, add milk and season well with salt and pepper. Dip squares into egg mixture and then in cracker crumbs. Fry in deep hot fat.

DIXIE CORN FRITTERS

1¾ cups flour
2 teaspoons baking powder
¾ teaspoon salt
1 egg, beaten
¾ cup milk
1 cup corn kernels, drained
1 tablespoon butter, melted
Vegetable oil

Sift flour, baking powder, and salt together. Combine egg, milk, corn and butter; stir into flour mixture. Pour vegetable oil into frying pan to a depth of 1 inch; heat. Drop batter from tip of large spoon into hot fat and fry 4 to 5 minutes, or until golden brown, turning when brown on one side. Drain on brown paper. Makes about 8 fritters.

OKRA WITH TOMATOES

1 pound okra
1 small onion, minced
3 tablespoons bacon fat
Salt and pepper

1 cup canned whole tomatoes
1 tablespoon chopped parsley

Wash okra, cut off stems. Slice. Brown onion in bacon fat. Add okra and cook for three minutes. Place in a baking dish, season and pour tomatoes over it. Sprinkle with parsley and bake in 350 degree oven for 30 minutes, or until done. Makes 6 servings.

SOUTHERN PECAN PIE

1 cup sugar
½ cup corn syrup
¼ cup butter, melted
3 eggs, well beaten
1 cup pecans, broken
1 pie shell, unbaked

Mix sugar, syrup and butter; add eggs and pecans. Fill unbaked pie shell with mixture and bake for 10 minutes at 400 degrees, then for 30 to 35 minutes at 350 degrees. Serve either cold or hot. Delicious topped with whipped cream.

A Midwestern Menu

❖ ❖ ❖ ❖ ❖ ❖ ❖ ❖

Potato Soup or French Pea Soup

Hot Rolls

Irish Stew

Cole Slaw

Danish Apple Cake

Coffee or Tea

Potato Soup

4 slices lean bacon, diced
6 leeks, thinly sliced
¼ cup chopped onion
2 tablespoons flour
4 cups chicken broth
3 large potatoes, thinly sliced
2 egg yolks, beaten
1 cup sour cream
3 tablespoons chopped parsley

Saute bacon in deep saucepan for 5 minutes. Add leeks and onion and saute for 5 minutes. Stir in flour. Slowly add chicken broth, stirring constantly. Add potatoes and simmer for 1 hour. Mix in blender or food processor until creamy. Combine egg yolks and sour cream. Add to soup. Simmer for 10 minutes, stirring constantly. Garnish with choppped fresh parsley. Makes about 2 quarts.

French Pea Soup

2 quarts water
2 cups green split peas
  Cooked ham bone
2 stalks celery, chopped
2 carrots, chopped

1 onion, chopped
¼ teaspoon thyme
¼ teaspoon marjoram
   Dash cayenne
·1 bay leaf
   Salt and pepper to taste

Combine ingredients, cover, and boil for 20 minutes. Then reduce heat and simmer about 40 minutes longer, until peas are done. Discard ham bone. Force remaining ingredients through coarse wire strainer and serve with croutons on top. Makes 8 servings.

TOURTIERE PIE

1½ pounds fresh pork, ground coarsely
1   medium-size onion, ground fine
⅛   teaspoon cinnamon
⅛   teaspoon crushed cloves
¼   teaspoon summer savory
¼   teaspoon sage
½   teaspoon salt
⅛   teaspoon pepper
    Pastry for 2 crusts

Mix pork, onion, and spices together and put into pastry-lined pie tin. Top with second crust and seal edges. Prick top crust and bake for 1 hour in hot oven (400 degrees).

31

SWEDISH MEAT BALLS

⅔ cup bread crumbs
1½ cups milk
1 medium onion, chopped fine
4 tablespoons butter, divided
¾ pound beef, ground
¾ pound pork, ground
1 egg
2 teaspoons salt
¼ teaspoon pepper
½ cup sherry

Soak bread crumbs in milk. Saute chopped onion in 1 tablespoon butter until slightly brown. Add meat, onion, unbeaten egg and seasonings to bread crumb mixture. Mix thoroughly.

Melt another tablespoon butter in skillet. Form small meat balls by scooping up some of the meat on a teaspoon which has been dipped into the hot fat (good Swedish cooks always do this so meat slips off spoon easily). Brown meat evenly, in batches. Keep shaking skillet to make meat balls turn over and over.

As each batch is nicely brown and thoroughly cooked, transfer to a plate, add butter to skillet and brown additional meat balls until all are cooked.

Add about ½ cup water to skillet, add sherry and all the meat balls. Cook gently over low heat for about 15 minutes or until all the liquid is absorbed. Makes 6 to 8 servings.

PIGS' FEET STEW WITH DUMPLINGS

2-4 pigs' feet or pork hocks
  4 celery leaves
     Salt and pepper to taste
  1 onion, chopped

Dumplings

  1 cup flour
  2 teaspoons baking powder
  ½ teaspoon salt
  1 teaspoon butter
  ¼ cup cold water

Place pigs' feet in pan with celery leaves, salt, pepper, and onion. Cover with water and boil until meat is tender and separates from the bone easily. To make dumplings, sift together flour, baking powder and salt in mixing bowl. Rub in butter lightly until all is well blended. Add water and mix until dough will hold together. Drop dumplings by spoonfuls into stew, cover, and allow to boil for 10 minutes. Serve hot.

POTATO PANCAKES

6 large potatoes, peeled and finely grated
4 eggs, beaten
2 tablespoons flour
1 teaspoon salt
   Dash of pepper
½ cup vegetable oil

Place grated potato pulp in cheesecloth and press out all excess water. Put potatoes into mixing bowl, add remaining ingredients except oil, and mix well. Heat oil in skillet. Drop mixture by tablespoon into hot oil and smooth into patties. Fry until both sides are golden brown. Serve with applesauce.

SWEET AND SOUR CABBAGE

4 cups shredded cabbage
4 slices bacon, diced

2 tablespoons brown sugar
1 tablespoon flour
½ cup water
⅓ cup vinegar
  Salt
  Pepper
2 cloves
1 small onion, sliced

Cook cabbage in boiling, salted water 7 minutes. Fry bacon. Add sugar and flour to bacon fat; blend. Add water, vinegar, and seasonings; cook until thick. Add onion, diced bacon, and cabbage; heat through. Makes 6 servings.

IRISH STEW

3 pounds lamb, cut in pieces
½ cup diced carrots
½ cup diced turnips
1 celery stalk, diced
1 onion, sliced
4 cups potatoes cut in ½ inch cubes
¼ cup flour
  Salt
  Pepper

Place meat in kettle, cover with boiling water, and cook slowly 2 hours or until tender. After cooking 1 hour, add carrots, turnips, celery, and onion. Half an hour before serving, add potatoes. Thicken with flour mixed with ¼ cup cold water. Season with salt and pepper. Serve with dumplings. Makes 8 servings.

COLE SLAW

	Garlic clove
2 to 3	cups shredded cabbage
½	cup sour cream
2	tablespoons sugar
¼	teaspoon salt
⅛	teaspoon celery salt
	Paprika
2	tablespoons vinegar

Rub bowl with garlic for flavor and put cabbage in bowl. Add seasonings to sour cream and mix well. Stir in vinegar gradually. (Makes about ⅔ cup dressing.) Pour dressing over cabbage and toss together lightly. Makes 6 servings.

HOT POTATO SALAD

8	medium potatoes
	Salt and pepper
½	cup diced celery

1 tablespoon finely chopped parsley
1 teaspoon caraway seed
3 tablespoons tarragon vinegar
2 tablespoons cider vinegar
4 tablespoons olive oil
1 slice lemon, ⅓ inch thick

Boil potatoes, cool, and slice into baking dish. Sprinkle with salt, pepper, celery, parsley, and caraway seed. Mix vinegars and oil, add lemon, and heat to boiling point, pour over potatoes, cover, and heat in 350 degree oven until warmed through. Makes 8 servings.

DANISH APPLE CAKE

1 package zwieback
1 cup sugar
½ cup butter
8 tart apples, pared, cored and sliced
½ cup heavy cream, whipped

Crush or grind zwieback and mix with sugar. Brown butter slowly in heavy frying pan. Do not burn. Stir into crumb mixture. Cover bottom of greased casserole with layer of crumbs; cover with sliced apples. Repeat layers of crumbs and apples until all are used, finishing with layer of crumbs on top. Bake in 325 degree oven for 1¼ hours, or until crusty. Serve with cream. Makes 8 servings.

SWEDISH PANCAKES

    3 eggs, separated
    2 tablespoons sugar
    ⅛ teaspoon salt
    3 tablespoons butter, melted
    ½ cup sifted flour
    1½ cups milk
       Lingonberry preserves
       Powdered sugar

Beat egg yolks with sugar, salt and melted butter. Stir in, alternately, flour and milk. Mix well. Let stand in a cool place until ready to use. Then whip egg whites until stiff and mix into batter.

Grease heated Swedish pancake pan or ordinary skillet with melted butter and pour or spoon a little batter for each pancake. Pancake browns almost at once. Turn pancake and let other side brown. Lift cakes to

warmed plates, arranging them 5 or 7
on a plate, in circle; spoon lingonber-
ry preserves in middle. Sprinkle cakes
with powdered sugar and serve.
Makes 2 dozen or more cakes.

SWEDISH SPRITZ COOKIES

1½ cups butter
1   cup sugar
1   well-beaten egg
2   teaspoons vanilla
4   cups flour
1   teaspoon baking powder

Thoroughly cream butter and sugar;
add egg and vanilla. Beat well. Add
sifted dry ingredients, mix to smooth
dough. Force through cookie press,
forming various shapes, or roll and
slice. Bake in hot oven (400 degrees)
until light brown—about 8 to 10 minutes.

A SOUTHWESTERN MENU

❖ ❖ ❖ ❖ ❖ ❖ ❖ ❖

GUACAMOLE WITH CORN CHIPS

CHILI CON CARNE AND/OR TACOS

REFRIED BEANS

TOSSED SALAD

FLAN OR SOPAIPILLAS

COFFEE OR TEA

GUACAMOLE

2 avocados
1 tomato, chopped
½ onion, minced
1 tablespoon lime or lemon juice
¼ teaspoon garlic salt
Salt and pepper

If avocados are hard when you buy them in the store, allow to ripen (not in the refrigerator!) until they begin to feel a little bit soft to the touch. Cut in half, remove stones, and mash up avocado meat with rest of ingredients. Use as party dip with corn chips or tortilla chips, or use as garnish on any salad. Dabs of guacamole may be topped with a teaspoonful of sour cream sprinkled with paprika for added decoration.

CHILI CON CARNE

½ cup sliced onions
1 clove garlic, chopped
3 tablespoons bacon fat
2 pounds ground beef
1½ cups canned tomatoes
2 cans red kidney beans

Salt
2 tablespoons chili powder
½ bay leaf

Fry onion and garlic in bacon fat. When partly done add beef and brown well. Place beef and onions in a large pot and add tomatoes and kidney beans. Season with salt and chili powder. Add bay leaf. Cook slowly for 1 to 1½ hours. Makes 8 servings.

TACOS

6 taco shells
½ pound grated Longhorn Cheddar cheese
½ head shredded iceberg lettuce

Filling

1 pound ground chuck
½ teaspoon cumin powder
1 teaspoon chili powder
Salt to taste
½ cup tomato sauce

Brown meat in heavy skillet with seasonings. Pour off fat. Add sauce and heat. Keep warm.

Salsa for Topping

3   peeled and chopped tomatoes
2   diced onions
3   diced green chili peppers

Combine ingredients.

Fill each taco shell with meat mixture. Sprinkle with cheese. Add lettuce and spoon on salsa.

PICANTE SAUCE

1   can tomato sauce
1   large fresh tomato, diced
½   teaspoon dried taco sauce mix
1   small can diced green chilis
1   can Spanish-style tomato sauce
1   bunch green onions, chopped
½   teaspoon or more crushed dried red
    peppers

Combine all ingredients and serve with tortilla or corn chips.

TEXAS CHILI CON CARNE

2   pounds stew meat, cut in ½ inch cubes
    (not ground)
1   large yellow onion, cut up
1   head garlic (10-12 cloves), minced

3-5 tablespoons chili powder
2 tablespoons ground comino
1 teaspoon salt
½ teaspoon black pepper
⅔ large can of tomato juice
⅓ large can of water

Brown meat in cast iron skillet or pot. Add seasonings, onion and garlic. Mix well. Add water and tomato juice and bring to boil. Lower heat and simmer for two hours, stirring every 5 minutes. Cool, refrigerate overnight. Reheat and serve with pinto beans and warmed corn tortillas. May be served with fresh, finely chopped onion, if desired. While cooking, be sure to stir about every 5-10 minutes, in order not to burn or scorch the chili. This recipe can be made in crock-pot or microwave successfully by lessening the amount of water and tomato juice added in the beginning since in a crock-pot or microwave the water does not evaporate to the extent it does on the stove. Chili con carne reheats very well in the microwave, and the crock-pot is an ideal way to serve the dish, particularly for buffet service.

William Elton Green

BARBECUE SAUCE

1 cup ketchup or tomato sauce
2 teaspoons chili powder
⅓ cup Worcestershire sauce
2 tablespoons lemon juice
2 teaspoons salt
¼ cup chopped onion
1 tablespoon brown sugar
2 garlic cloves, minced
2 cups water
2 tablespoons butter

Combine all ingredients and bring to a boil.

Mary L. Williams

PINYON NUT TURKEY STUFFING

⅓ cup butter
1 medium onion, chopped
½ cup mushrooms, sliced
4 cups bread crumbs
1 teaspoon salt
½ teaspoon pepper
½ teaspoon crumbled wild sage
1 egg, beaten
2 cups pinyon nuts, shelled and roasted

Melt butter in skillet, add onion and mushrooms, and saute 5 minutes. Add crumbs, seasonings, egg and pinyon nuts. Toss to mix thoroughly. Fill cavity of turkey with stuffing.

REFRIED PINTO BEANS

4 tablespoons minced onion
2 tablespoons bacon fat
2 cups pinto beans, cooked
4 tablespoons grated Cheddar cheese

Saute onion in bacon fat. Mash cold cooked beans and add to onion, stirring constantly until completely dry. Add cheese while cooking beans slowly.

BAKING POWDER BISCUITS

2 cups flour
4 teaspoons baking powder
½ teaspoon salt
3 tablespoons shortening
½ cup milk

Mix and sift dry ingredients. Cut in shortening. Add milk to make soft dough. Toss onto slightly floured board and knead to make mixture smooth. Roll lightly until dough is about ½ inch thick. Cut with biscuit cutter. Place in biscuit pan. Bake at 450 degrees for 15 minutes.

SOPAIPILLAS

4 cups flour
1 teaspoon salt
1¾ cups lukewarm water
3 teaspoons baking powder
¼ cup sugar
   Cooking oil for frying

Combine all ingredients to form sticky dough. Put one-quarter of the dough onto floured board and knead until smooth and not sticky. Pat into rectangle about one-quarter inch thick. Cut into diamond shapes and cut 2 slashes into each piece, so that when it is fried it looks somewhat like a pretzel. Deep fry on both sides until golden. Repeat procedure with remaining dough. Dip in honey or a mixture of cinnamon and sugar.

FLAN

6 egg yolks
¼ cup sugar
1 cup milk
1 cup light cream
¾ teaspoon vanilla
⅛ teaspoon salt

Beat egg yolks, then stir in rest of ingredients. Put 6 custard cups in baking dish, sides of which are higher than cups, then pour boiling water into dish until water level reaches 1 inch. Pour custard mixture into cups, and bake at 350 degrees for about 30 minutes, or until knife inserted into custard comes out clean. Serve either hot or cold.

PEACH COBBLER

Topping

1 cup sifted flour
1 tablespoon sugar
1½ teaspoons baking powder
½ teaspoon salt
3 tablespoons shortening
½ cup light cream

Filling

  4 cups fresh, drained canned, or frozen
     peaches
⅓ cup sugar
  1 tablespoon flour

Mix dry ingredients and shortening thoroughly. Mix in cream. Grease 8-inch baking dish with butter and cut up peaches into it. Add sugar and flour. Drop topping onto peaches by spoonfuls until dough almost covers dish. Bake for 20 minutes in a 400 degree oven.

APPLE FRITTERS

  4 large tart apples
½ cup flour
½ teaspoon baking powder
  1 tablespoon melted butter
½ teaspoon salt
  1 egg
½ cup cold water
     Butter for frying

Peel, core, and cut apples into thick slices. Mix flour, baking powder, melted butter, and salt. Break egg into cold water and beat until foamy. Add this to flour and mix into a batter. Dip apple slices into batter. Fry in butter.

A Western Menu

❖❖❖❖❖❖❖❖

Avocado Curry Soup

Sourdough Biscuits

Broiled Salmon Steaks
With Mustard Sauce

Fried Tomatoes

Fresh Coconut Pie

Coffee or Tea

Avocado Curry Soup

      1   tablespoon butter
      1   teaspoon curry
1½   cups chicken consomme
      1   cup cream
      1   slightly beaten egg yolk
      1   medium-size avocado, peeled and
           seeded

Melt butter, stir in curry and add consomme. Bring to boil; cover and simmer 10 minutes. Combine cream with
egg yolk and gradually stir into soup.
Mash half avocado; dice other half;
add both to soup. Heat, stirring constantly. Serve hot or cold. Makes 5
servings.

Sourdough Starter

2   cups lukewarm potato water
2   cups flour
1   tablespoon sugar

First make potato water by cutting up
2 medium potatoes into cubes and
boiling in 3 cups of water until tender. Remove potatoes and measure out

2 cups of remaining liquid. Mix potato water, flour and sugar into a smooth paste. Set in a warm place until starter mixture rises to double its original size.

SOURDOUGH BISCUITS

3 to 4 cups sifted flour
1 cup sourdough starter
1 teaspoon salt
1 teaspoon sugar
1 teaspoon baking soda
1 tablespoon shortening
Melted shortening

Place flour in a bowl, make a well in the center, and add sourdough starter (above). Stir in salt, sugar and soda, and add 1 tablespoon shortening. Gradually mix in enough flour to make a stiff dough. Pinch off dough for one biscuit at a time; form a ball and roll it in melted shortening. Crowd biscuits in a round 8-inch cake pan and allow to rise in a warm place for 20 to 30 minutes before baking. Bake at 425 degrees until done.

Chicken and Avocado Salad

    3   avocados
         Fresh lemon juice
         Salt
    2   cups cubed cooked chicken
  1½   cups diced celery
    ½   cup slivered toasted almonds
    1   cup mayonnaise
    1   teaspoon mustard

Halve, seed and peel avocados. Sprinkle with lemon juice and salt. Combine chicken, celery, almonds, mayonnaise and mustard. Top avocado halves with chicken mixture. Makes 6 servings.

Fried Abalone

    8   slices abalone
         Salt
         Pepper
    2   eggs, beaten
         Bread crumbs
         Butter

Pound slices of abalone vigorously with wooden mallet. Wipe dry, sprinkle with salt and pepper, dip into well-beaten egg and then into bread crumbs. Brown quickly in butter allowing not more than 1½ to 2 minutes to each side. Serve immediately. No sauce is needed.

BROILED SALMON STEAKS

8 salmon steaks
  Juice of 1 lemon
  Flour for dredging
  Salt
  Paprika
  Salad oil

Sprinkle salmon steaks generously with lemon juice. Flour one side only. Place floured side down in pre-heated broiler pan containing enough oil to cover bottom of pan. Turn immediately. Sprinkle with salt and paprika and broil until well browned without further turning, or about 12 minutes. Makes 8 servings.

SALMON SAUCE

4 egg yolks
1 cup olive oil
2 tablespoons vinegar

3 teaspoons French mustard
2 teaspoons English mustard
½ cup finely chopped dill
1 teaspoon salt
½ teaspoon pepper
3 teaspoons sugar

Beat egg yolks with oil; gradually add vinegar, a few drops at a time, beating steadily. Beat in mustards and dill, then salt, pepper and sugar. Mix well and chill. Makes 8 or more servings.

PORK WITH CELLOPHANE NOODLES

1 2-ounce package cellophane noodles
½ pound ground pork
3 tablespoons peanut oil
2 tablespoons sherry
1 teaspoon salt
½ teaspoon sugar
2 tablespoons dark soy sauce
½ cup minced water chestnuts
½ cup chicken broth

Soak noodles in hot water for 30 minutes. Drain and cut into 2-inch pieces. Stir fry pork in oil for 3 minutes, until well cooked. Add sherry, salt, sugar, and soy sauce. Mix well. Add water chestnuts and mix again. Add noodles. Stir a few times and add broth. Cook until mixture is almost dry.

SHRIMP TEMPURA

18 large shrimp
2 cups flour
¼ cup cornstarch
½ teaspoon baking powder
1 lightly beaten egg
Salt to taste
1¼ cups cold water

Peel shrimp, leaving tails intact. Cut shrimp lengthwise about ¾ through; do not cut into tail sections. Carefully remove any large veins. Rinse under cold water. Drain and pat dry.

Place flour, cornstarch and baking powder in a mixing bowl. Stir in egg and salt. Add water. Stir lightly. Batter should be a little lumpy.

Pour fat to a depth of one inch into a skillet and heat to 375 degrees. Dip shrimp in batter and drop, one at a time, into hot fat and cook, turning once or twice, until golden brown.

Walnut Chicken

2 pounds boned and skinned chicken breasts
½ tablespoon cornstarch
½ teaspoon salt
1 tablespoon Shaohing wine
4 tablespoons oil, divided
½ teaspoon powdered ginger
Dash pepper
½ teaspoon sugar
1 cup coarsely chopped walnuts

Dice chicken. Combine with cornstarch, salt and wine. Sauté chicken in 3 tablespoons oil for 3 minutes. Season with ginger, pepper and sugar. Stir until chicken is done. Allow chicken to cool slightly. In a separate pan, fry walnuts in remaining oil. Add walnuts to chicken and serve.

Carne Oja (Beef Cooked in a Pot)

3 carrots
1 large onion
1 plate of beef ribs, split lengthwise (ask your butcher)
4 cloves garlic, chopped

1 chili pepper, small jalapeno, or larger red
  chili
1 teaspoon whole allspice
½ teaspoon whole cloves
1 tablespoon salt
1 teaspoon fresh-ground pepper or 1
  tablespoon whole peppercorns
  A few sprigs fresh cilantro
1 tablespoon dried oregano
2 8-ounce cans garbanzo beans
1 head green cabbage

Slice carrots into chunks and quarter
onion. Put beef, onion, carrots, garlic,
chili, spices and herbs into a pot, add
water to half-cover contents, cover,
and simmer for one hour. Add gar-
banzos, top off with more water if
necessary, cover, and simmer for another ½ hour. Quarter cabbage and
place on top of meat; cook an additional 20 minutes, or until cabbage is
just tender. Makes 6 generous servings. (Leftover broth makes delicious
soup.)

FRIED TOMATOES

4 large tomatoes
  Bread crumbs
  Salt and pepper

1   egg, beaten
    Vegetable shortening

Wash and cut tomatoes in slices about ½ inch thick. Season bread crumbs with salt and pepper. Dip tomatoes in well-beaten egg and then in crumbs. Fry in hot shortening until golden brown. Makes 6 servings.

Fresh Coconut Pie

2   cups coconut, freshly grated
2   cups milk
¼   cup coconut milk
½   cup sugar
5   tablespoons flour
2   tablespoons cornstarch
¼   teaspoon salt
3   egg yolks, beaten
½   teaspoon vanilla
½   teaspoon lemon extract
1   drop almond extract
1   baked pie shell
½   pint cream, whipped

Scald 1 cup of coconut with milk and coconut milk in double boiler about 20 minutes; strain; discard this coconut. Return milk to double boiler. Mix